Always plead the fifth!

I DON'T ANSWER QUESTIONS!

Pleading the Fifth!

David G. Ridings

THE AUTHOR

David Ridings has spent his entire adult life on every side of the criminal justice system. When he was a young man, he first became interested in police work when he would see officers stationed at crime scenes, or on a traffic stop. He would always wonder what was going on at those crime or traffic scenes. And, he would think to himself, "that guy (the police officer) knows exactly what's going on. He is so lucky." And ultimately, he decided that he wanted to be involved on that level. He always wanted to be the one who was "in the know". So, he set out to become a police officer.

In the 1980's David went to college to learn as much as he could about the legal system. He majored in Criminal Justice Administration, with a minor in Sociology and Psychology. He got his master's degree in the same area, and then set off to put his education into experience. He became a police officer.

In 1987 David became an intern with the Tennessee Bureau of Investigation traveling all over the state in the Governor's Task Force on Marijuana Eradication. Later, in 1989 David became a police officer in Murfreesboro Tennessee and worked the patrol section. In 1990 David transferred to Metro Nashville Police Department. He spent most of that time working the streets of Nashville as a patrol officer in the inner city. He later worked in an "undercover" capacity as a police officer investigating street crime and drug sales. And while he was a police officer, he went to Law School at night. In approximately 1996, David published his thesis on Community Policing, while working on his master's degree (and in Law School simultaneously).

In 1997, his last year in law school, David got licensed to practice law one year early under the special supreme court rule to practice law under the supervision of Davidson County District Attorney Victor "Torry" Johnson. As an intern at the DA's office prosecuting criminal offenses, David was able to see the next level up from being a police officer. He was able to work directly in the legal system prosecuting these cases in court that he had been previously producing as an officer on the streets.

In 1998, he opened his own law firm in the heart of Nashville, and quickly because one of the premiere Criminal Defense Attorney's in Nashville because of his unique experience on every side of the law. Today Mr. Ridings continues that practice, with some additional trial experience under his belt, and teaches other lawyers in CLE's (continuing legal education courses).

Recently Mr. Ridings was appointed by the eleven General Sessions Court Judges to be a Special Night Court Magistrate. He works part-time in this capacity sitting "special" for the full-time night court magistrate's when they take off work. He still operates his criminal defense firm and does the parttime magistrate work only when needed when the full-time magistrates take off and need a replacement. But this gives Mr. Ridings a unique advantage in defending his clients and walking them through (quite literally) every stage of the criminal justice process as someone who has been there, done that, and (now) written the book!

Today you can read the book written by the only lawyer who could write the book based upon experience that he didn't get from a book. Now… say that three times real fast!

ACKNOWLEDGMENTS

"David Glenn Ridings, you could argue with a fence post." There is no telling how many times I have heard these words (and using my middle name, no less). I want to thank my parents Ted and Mary Ridings, for the inspiration that it took to finally get me to go to law school. While I didn't always listen (and I did argue... a lot), eventually your sound advice and loving inspiration paid off.

To my wife, Lynda. What a joy you are with which to do life. There are not words sufficient to describe my love and respect for you. You are truly the best thing that ever happened to me. You lift me up when I need lifting... and you put me in my place equally as often. I could not be the man I am today without you. We were truly made for each other!

To my children and now grandchildren. You have become what drives me to be, not only successful, but also a man of integrity. I want you all to be able to say, "I'm proud of him".

PREFACE

As an attorney I find most of my clients are very good people who were raised to respect authority. They find themselves in unfortunate situations and some of the most stressful times of their lives. Invariably, I teach people in our first consultation what they wish they would have known the day before they got arrested. It is always disheartening to see these good people give up their constitutional rights, and make mistakes in talking to the police, simply because they wanted to "cooperate". And simply because society has taught them the wrong way to "cooperate" their entire life.

People are taught from an early age that:

- The policeman is your friend.
- Cops are here to help and protect you.
- When you are in trouble, look for a policeman.
- Cooperate with the police whenever you can.
- Cops are good.

And, while on some level those are (basically) true statements…they are not "always" true. And they are not always exclusive or absolute.

In fact, sometimes police are trained to trick you into confessing to your involvement in a particular activity. Sometimes the job of a policeman is to arrest you, convict you, and ultimately lock you up in jail. Sometimes calling the police into a family situation (an argument or disagreement with a friend or family member) is the absolute WORST thing you can do. Because, when you drill down to it, sometimes the police officers' job is to take your liberty and deprive you of your freedom. And it is in those times that I want to teach people a better way to deal with police contact.

I have often said "when you invite the government into your life, it is hard to get them to leave". And make no mistake here; the "police department" IS "the government".

People (in general) are raised to respect authority. They are raised to believe "cops are your friend" and you can "trust" them. And over the years my opinion on these matters has taken a different view, depending on the "side" I was on. I have spent over a decade in some form of law enforcement roll. Protecting. Serving. Arresting. And Prosecuting. I can tell you from working on that side that it is MUCH easier to prosecute someone who doesn't resist. It is easier to "convict" someone who "admits" the wrongdoing. It is easier to win the case if you can get the person to confess the things that would otherwise be hard for you to prove. Work smarter, not harder, we would say.

I meet so many people who say things like "well, they knew I was the driver even though they didn't see me drive because I was the only person there". Or "they knew I had been drinking because they could smell it. So, I admitted drinking". Or "I was just cooperating with the police" (when I gave up my right to remain silent and, basically told it all). "They were going to find my weed anyway, so I just told them where it was". Or "they would have found out anyway."

I always remind people: what the police "know" and what they are "able to prove" are two very different things. So, make them do their job. Make them do whatever it takes to prove you were the one driving. Make them do what is required to get a search warrant for your blood. Make the police officer do his or her job. Period. That way you at least leave something for your lawyer to argue about. That's what we do best! Argue! And we LOVE to do it!

DISCLAIMER

The information in this book is not intended to be legal advice in any way. It does not create, nor does it attempt to create an attorney/client relationship. The information in this book is for entertainment purposes and provides the reader basic information of which I have become aware over years of practice and experience on every side of the law. If you have the need or desire for legal advice, you should contact an attorney immediately. Do not seek legal advice in this book! Read it for fun and educate yourself. THEN… go teach others what you have learned.

TABLE OF CONTENTS

Introduction	1
Chapter 1. The Foundations of Justice	5
The United States Constitution: A Beacon of Rights	5
The Fifth Amendment: The Right to Remain Silent	6
Miranda v. Arizona (384 U.S. 436, 1966)	8
The Sixth Amendment: The Right To Counsel	10
Gideon v. Wainwright (372 U.S. 335, 1963)	10
Chapter 2. The Power of Silence	13
The Psychology of Police Interrogations	14
The Risk of Self-Incrimination	14
The Erosion of Witness Credibility	15
Real-life Examples: The Consequences of Ignoring Silence	16
In Conclusion	17
Chapter 3. Miranda Rights: The Gateway to Silence	19
The Evolution of the Miranda Warning	19
Understanding the Right to Counsel	20
The Role of Custody and Interrogation	20
Rhode Island v. Innis (446 U.S. 291, 1980)	21
Chapter 4. The Thin Line Between Cooperation and Compulsion	23
The Perils of Voluntary Statements	24
The Impact of Deceptive Police Tactics	24
The Duty of Law Enforcement to Respect Rights	25
Miranda v. Arizona (384 U.S. 436, 1966)	25
Missouri v. Seibert (542 U.S. 600, 2004)	26
In Conclusion	27

Chapter 5. The Attorney's Role in Protecting Silence   29
    The Sixth Amendment and Right to Legal Counsel   29
    Safeguarding Clients During Interrogations   30
    Effective Legal Representation in Action?   31
    Did this guy do the right thing or not?   32

Chapter 6. The Tennessee Constitution and Your Rights   37
    The State's Duty to Protect Individual Rights   37
    Article I, Section 9: Protections against Self-Incrimination   38
    A Comparative Analysis: U.S. vs. Tennessee Constitution   39

Chapter 7. Practical Wisdom: Navigating Police Encounters   43
    Do's and Don'ts When Confronted by Law Enforcement   43
    The Importance of Legal Literacy in Society   47
    DUI Investigations Specifically   48

Chapter 8. Real Life: True Stories from my Law Practice   53
    Case Number One   54
    Case Number Two   56
    Case Number Three   57
    Case Number Four   61
    Case Number Five   62
    Case Number Six   63

Chapter 9. What now?   69
    Educating the Public on Their Rights   69
    Your Responsibility   71

CONCLUSION   73

INTRODUCTION

In a society where justice is sought and safeguarded, silence emerges as a potent weapon to protect one's rights and preserve the integrity of the legal system. And the power of that "silence" is often underestimated. This book explores the constitutional foundations of silence, the psychological nuances of police interrogations, and the impact of landmark legal cases on the right to remain silent. By embracing the massive power of silence, individuals can empower themselves to navigate the criminal justice system with prudence, protect their constitutional rights, and ensure that justice prevails. If you follow the basic premise laid out in this book, you will always *leave room for your rights*! (So-to-speak).

As a former police officer, prosecutor, and now a Judicial Magistrate and criminal defense attorney, I have witnessed the pivotal role that remaining silent plays in protecting individuals' constitutional rights and ensuring a fair legal process.

I have always wanted to write this book, and teach people what they wish they had known the day before they got arrested. This book delves deep into the importance of maintaining silence and the reasons why individuals should never speak to the police without the guidance of legal counsel. Through a comprehensive exploration of the United States and Tennessee Constitutions, along with analysis of landmark legal cases, this book aims to empower readers with the knowledge they need to safeguard their rights and navigate the criminal justice system.

"I don't answer questions" (without a lawyer) is the ONLY thing you should ever say to a police officer. Period. Full stop! Read on, and let's learn why.

Chapter 1

THE FOUNDATIONS OF JUSTICE

In the intricate tapestry of a just society, the United States Constitution stands as a beacon, guiding the path to fairness, liberty, and the protection of individual rights. Rooted in the profound belief that justice is the cornerstone of any civilized nation, the Constitution weaves a narrative of fundamental principles that safeguard the rights of its citizens. This chapter delves into the cornerstone of these principles, focusing on the Fifth and Sixth Amendments to the United States Constitution, two essential pillars that ensure the balance between the rights of individuals and the needs of society.

The United States Constitution: A Beacon of Rights

When the framers of the United States Constitution embarked on their monumental task, they were driven by the conviction that a just government must protect and empower its people. Enshrined within this sacred document are the ideals that have continued to shape the nation's identity and destiny. The Constitution stands as a testament to the principle that justice is not just an abstract concept but a tangible, guiding force that underpins every aspect of life on earth, and the governance of its people. It truly is a brilliant document.

The Fifth Amendment: The Right to Remain Silent

Embedded within the US Constitution, specifically in the Fifth Amendment lies a shield that safeguards individual citizens of this country from self-incrimination. This is a staple in American justice, and an incredible form of protection for the people of the United States.

The Fifth Amendment specifically says:

No person shall be held to answer for a capital, or otherwise infamous crime, unless on a presentment or indictment of a grand jury, except in cases arising in the land or naval forces, or in the militia, when in actual service in time of war or public danger; nor shall any person be subject for the same offense to be twice put in jeopardy of life or limb; nor shall be compelled in any criminal case to be a witness against himself, nor be deprived of life, liberty, or property, without due process of law; nor shall private property be taken for public use, without just compensation.

The Fifth Amendment encompasses several important rights, including:

1. **Protection against Double Jeopardy:** It prevents a person from being tried twice for the same crime after being acquitted or convicted, ensuring that individuals are not subjected to multiple prosecutions for the same offense. Remind me to tell you the story of when I got thrown in jail by a Judge for reminding him about the rules on double jeopardy and pulling what he called a "sneaky big-city-lawyer trick" to get the case dismissed. Now that was a fun Friday!

2. **Protection against Self-Incrimination:** The "right to remain silent" clause ensures that individuals cannot be compelled to testify against themselves in a criminal case. This is where the concept of "pleading the Fifth" comes from.

3. **Right to Due Process:** It guarantees that individuals cannot be deprived of life, liberty, or property without "due process of law." This means that legal procedures must be fair and follow established rules. It is what we "lawyers" work so hard to protect.

4. **Grand Jury Indictment:** Serious criminal charges generally require a grand jury indictment, a formal accusation of a crime issued by a grand jury. The grand jury meets in secret. It was formed in the days of the King as a secret group that would meet and tell the King about problems in his kingdom. (I could write a whole book alone about the grand jury, but we will save that for another day).

5. **Eminent Domain:** The "just compensation" clause ensures that if the government takes private property for

public use through eminent domain, the property owner must receive fair compensation. This is not a subject for this book, but it goes to show you that the Fifth Amendment encompasses a lot.

These protections are fundamental to the rights of individuals in the United States and are intended to safeguard against potential abuses of power by the government in criminal proceedings.

This right further ensures that no person can be compelled to bear witness against themselves in a criminal case, reflecting the acknowledgment that justice must be pursued through fair means. The idea that one should not be forced to contribute to their own prosecution underscores the system's commitment to uncovering truth without violating the dignity of the individual.

Miranda v. Arizona (384 U.S. 436, 1966)

In the annals of legal history, one case stands tall as a turning point in the protection of individual rights: Miranda v. Arizona. This landmark decision by the United States Supreme Court solidified the notion that suspects in custody *must be informed of their right to remain silent and the right to legal counsel.* This warning must be given by police BEFORE questioning that could put the person in peril of arrest. The ruling not only crystallized the significance of these rights but also recognized the inherent vulnerability of individuals subjected to police interrogation. "Mirandizing" suspects became a symbol of fairness, assuring that justice operates within the boundaries of respect for human rights.

But just because the court says the police must tell you about these rights, doesn't mean that your rights to remain silent "unless and until" they tell you. Your right to remain silent is absolute. And you should always do it, even if police don't remind you to do so.

Here are the specific rights that were formed by the litigation of Miranda vs. Arizona.

Miranda Warnings:

You have the right to remain silent. Anything you say can and will be used against you in a court of law. You have the right to an attorney, and to consult that attorney before any questions. If you cannot afford an attorney, one will be appointed to you at no cost to you. If you choose to answer questions, you have the right to stop answering questions at any time you wish, and invoke these rights. Do you understand these rights? And with these rights in mind, do you wish to speak with me?

They are taught in every police academy class in the country, and most U.S. citizens can even quote them almost verbatim. So you would think that more people would understand what they mean. But, no! That's exactly why I'm writing this book.

The Sixth Amendment: The Right To Counsel

At the heart of a just society lies the principle that every accused individual is entitled to a fair trial, with adequate legal representation. The Sixth Amendment guarantees the right to counsel, recognizing that the complexities of legal proceedings demand expertise beyond the reach of the average citizen. This fundamental right reaffirms the belief that justice cannot be served if one party lacks the means to effectively present their case.

The **Sixth Amendment** specifically says:

In all criminal prosecutions, the accused shall enjoy the right to a speedy and public trial, by an impartial jury of the State and district wherein the crime shall have been committed, which district shall have been previously ascertained by law, and to be informed of the nature and cause of the accusation; to be confronted with the witnesses against him; to have compulsory process for obtaining witnesses in his favor, and to have the Assistance of Counsel for his defense.

Gideon v. Wainwright (372 U.S. 335, 1963)

The case of Gideon v. Wainwright stands as a testament to the transformative power of the Sixth Amendment. In a unanimous decision, the Supreme Court held that states must provide legal counsel to indigent defendants accused of serious crimes. This ruling obliterated the barriers that had long prevented equal access to justice for all, regardless of economic status. Gideon's triumph not only reshaped the landscape of criminal justice but also reiterated the Constitution's commitment to fairness and due process.

In the grand saga of justice, the Fifth and Sixth Amendments are not mere legal doctrines; they are the bedrock upon which a just society stands. They remind us that justice is not a one-sided pursuit but a delicate balance between the rights of individuals and the collective well-being of society. Through landmark cases like **_Miranda v. Arizona_** and **_Gideon v. Wainwright_**, the United States legal system has fortified its commitment to protecting individual rights, ensuring that the quest for justice remains unwavering even as the tides of time and circumstance evolve.

Chapter 2

THE POWER OF SILENCE

In the hustle and bustle of today's fast-paced world, the potency of silence often goes unnoticed. Yet, in the realm of criminal justice, particularly during police interrogations, silence can speak volumes. This chapter will delve into the psychological aspects of police questioning, the perils of self-incrimination, and the diminishing trustworthiness of witnesses who are unable to maintain their quietude. Through real-life examples, we will further explore the repercussions of neglecting the power that silence wields.

In other words, most people in America know their Miranda Rights. Anyone who has even a modicum of experience or knowledge about these rights can quote them almost verbatim. But what most people don't know is "how" to invoke these rights, or why they are so important. The first right that came from Miranda is "the right to remail silent". But it is also the first right that people forget to protect. And, it's not easy. It takes a very specifically trained person to not give evidence against themselves when talking to the police. We want the readers of this book to be "that" specifically trained.

The Psychology of Police Interrogations

Interrogations are high-pressure situations where police officers employ a multitude of techniques to extract confessions or crucial information. Their tactics can range from building rapport, feigned empathy, to good-cop/bad-cop routines. At the heart of these methods lies the understanding of human psychology.

Silence, especially when prolonged, creates discomfort. In a room devoid of distractions, the eerie hush magnifies every heartbeat, every sigh, creating an ambiance of amplified tension. Humans naturally want to fill such voids. And it's this very instinct that interrogators bank on – the impulse to speak just to break the silence, even if it means divulging more than intended. Even if it means incriminating yourself.

The Risk of Self-Incrimination

In many legal systems, individuals have the right to remain silent to avoid self-incrimination. But why is this so important?

When individuals are under duress, especially in an interrogation setting, they might confess to crimes they haven't committed simply to end the pressure. Moreover, unintentional slips or improperly phrased statements can be twisted to fit a narrative, leading to false convictions. You think this cannot possibly happen, but there are thousands of examples to the contrary. And we want the reader of this book to be protected from that possibility.

The power of silence, in this context, acts as a safeguard. By choosing not to speak, one shields themselves from potential misinterpretations and the cunning strategies of seasoned interrogators.

The Erosion of Witness Credibility

Witnesses play a pivotal role in the legal process. Their testimonies can corroborate or challenge evidence, shaping the trajectory of a case. Yet, the reliability of a witness can be compromised if they fail to harness the power of silence. Their statements can be challenged for inconsistencies, and compared against previous statements.

When witnesses speak too much or provide inconsistent accounts, their credibility wanes. Each added detail, each revision to their statement, can be used to undermine their credibility and/or reliability. Often, defense attorneys will seize upon these inconsistencies, painting the witness as unreliable or biased.

In contrast, a witness who maintains consistent silence until the appropriate moment preserves their credibility and ensures their testimony holds more weight. If you are charged with a crime, and you refrain from making a statement until the actual jury trial, you cannot be tricked with questions about "changing" your statement. Your credibility cannot be challenged for making previous "inconsistent" statements. Because there are no previous statements. **Save your statement for when it counts!**

Real-life Examples: The Consequences of Ignoring Silence

Case 1: The Central Park Five - In 1989, five young men were wrongfully convicted for the assault and rape of a female jogger in New York's Central Park. Interrogation tactics, including prolonged periods of questioning without legal representation, led some of them to confess falsely. Their eagerness to end the interrogation overshadowed their right to silence, leading to years of imprisonment until their exoneration. Years later, the real culprit was convicted, and DNA matched this offender (but none of the other five men). It goes to show you that people can be tricked into confessing to crimes they did not commit. Scary. But true.

Case 2: Brendan Dassey - Featured in the documentary "Making a Murderer," Dassey's case highlights the dangers of speaking without understanding the implications. A young and impressionable Dassey was coaxed into providing a confession, which played a significant role in his conviction. The absence of silence and lack of legal counsel during crucial moments led to a controversial conviction.

Fun Fact: If you say something "against" your interest while being interrogated by police, it is admissible against you in a trial whether or not you testify. Conversely, if you say something "good" for your defense, or you "deny" your involvement the charges it is NOT admissible in court "unless" you testify. So, again, why on earth would you talk to the police? People make that mistake every single day!

In Conclusion

Silence is not merely the absence of sound; it's a potent tool in the realm of legal proceedings. Whether you're the accused, a witness, or merely an observer, recognizing the power of silence can drastically alter the course of justice. As the old adage goes, "Silence is golden," and nowhere is this more pertinent than in the corridors of justice (**or in the back seat of a police car**).

The People

Article 1

5th Amen

wer for a capital, or

jury, except

Chapter 3

MIRANDA RIGHTS: THE GATEWAY TO SILENCE

The Evolution of the Miranda Warning

At the heart of the American legal system lies a commitment to safeguarding an individual's constitutional rights, particularly when they are in their most vulnerable state – under arrest and facing police interrogation. The evolution of the Miranda Warning can be traced back to the landmark U.S. Supreme Court decision in Miranda v. Arizona (1966). Ernesto Miranda, a man accused of kidnapping and rape, confessed to the crimes without being informed of his right to remain silent or to have an attorney present during questioning. The Supreme Court ruled that the confession could not be used as evidence since Miranda was not informed of his rights, thus giving birth to the now-infamous Miranda Warning.

It is now a mandatory practice for law enforcement officers to relay these rights to individuals before custodial interrogations. The warning typically includes the right to remain silent, the fact that anything said can be used against the individual in court, the right to an attorney, and if the person cannot afford an attorney, one will be appointed.

Understanding the Right to Counsel

The right to counsel is enshrined in the Sixth Amendment of the U.S. Constitution. It ensures that individuals have the right to legal representation when facing criminal charges. This protection is designed to balance the scales of justice by providing individuals with a knowledgeable advocate to counter the power and resources of the state.

However, it wasn't until Gideon v. Wainwright (1963) that the Supreme Court mandated states to provide attorneys for defendants who could not afford one in felony cases. This underscored the importance of an individual's right to legal representation irrespective of their financial status.

The Role of Custody and Interrogation

For the Miranda Rights to be invoked, two primary conditions must be met: the individual must be in custody and subjected to interrogation. "Custody" is broadly defined as when a person is not free to leave the presence of law enforcement. "Interrogation" encompasses not just direct questioning but also any words or actions on the part of the police that the police should know are likely to elicit an incriminating response.

However, simply being in police custody does not necessitate a Miranda warning. It becomes essential only when an individual in custody is about to be interrogated. This distinction has led to numerous legal debates and court decisions aimed at clarifying the specifics of "custody" and "interrogation".

Rhode Island v. Innis (446 U.S. 291, 1980)

This case serves as a significant reference point in understanding the parameters of what constitutes an "interrogation." In Rhode Island v. Innis, Thomas Innis was arrested for robbery and murder. While being transported to the police station, officers discussed the presence of a shotgun near a school and the potential harm it could cause to children. Innis subsequently led the police to the weapon, even though he hadn't been directly questioned.

The Supreme Court had to decide whether the conversation between the officers amounted to an interrogation. It concluded that while the police officers did not directly question Innis, their conversation was designed to elicit a response from him. However, the court also stated that interrogation refers not only to express questioning but also to any practices that the police should know are likely to elicit an incriminating response. Thus, the court ruled in favor of the state, stating that Innis was not subjected to a police-initiated interrogation.

This decision is instrumental in shaping the understanding of indirect methods of questioning and their relationship with the Miranda Rights.

The chapter on Miranda Rights and their implications underscores their centrality in the American criminal justice system. These rights are not just legal technicalities; they serve as a fundamental safeguard for individual freedoms in the face of state power.

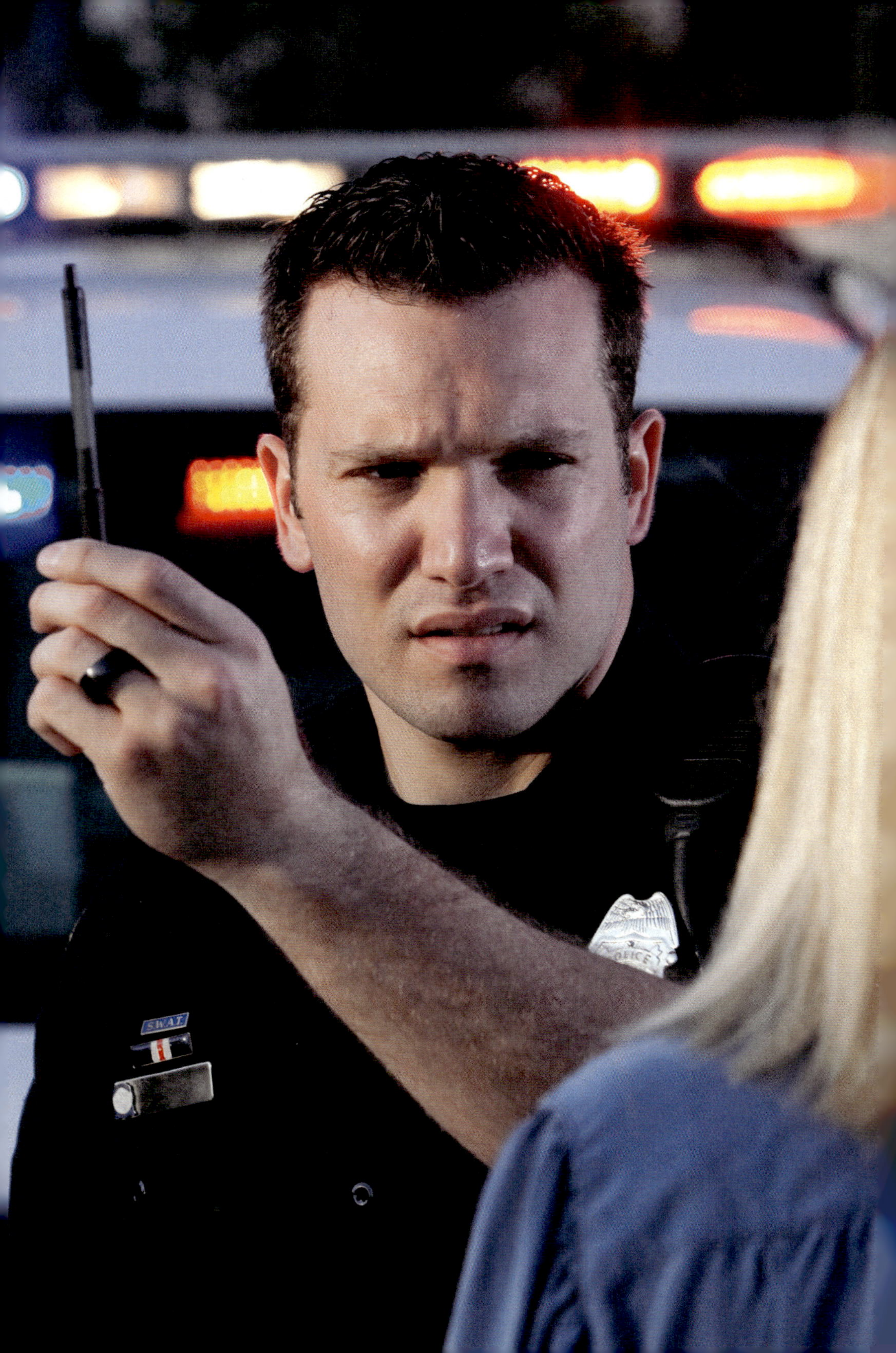
S.W.A.T.

Chapter 4

THE THIN LINE BETWEEN COOPERATION AND COMPULSION

So many times I hear from my clients "I just wanted to cooperate with the police". Or, in the process of cooperating with police, "I took those tests because I thought I had to take them". Cooperating with police means something totally different to me than it does to others. It does NOT mean giving up your rights.

Cooperating with police means saying "yes sir, or yes ma'am" or "no sir or no ma'am". It simply means being nice. Cooperating means when he tells you to get out of the car, you get out of the car. When he says "stand over there", you simply stand over there. But when the police start wanting you to take tests, or answer questions, you say "I don't answer questions without a lawyer". Or "I don't take tests without a lawyer".

When he says "where have you been tonight?" You say "I'm sorry officer, I don't answer questions without a lawyer". You absolutely have the right to do that.

The Perils of Voluntary Statements

At the heart of the justice system is the presumption of innocence, where every individual is deemed **innocent until proven guilty**. Integral to this process is the gathering of evidence, with statements made by the accused being among the most potent. Voluntary statements are often considered to be more genuine as they are made without any external pressures. However, what may seem voluntary at first glance may not be so straightforward.

Many individuals might provide voluntary statements under the impression that cooperating will make things easier for them. Yet, there exists a fine line between voluntarily cooperating and feeling compelled to do so due to perceived or actual pressure from law enforcement. Traversing this path is precarious, as these statements can inadvertently self-incriminate the individual, even if they are innocent.

The Impact of Deceptive Police Tactics

Deceptive police tactics have often been under the spotlight, with critics arguing they blur the line between cooperation and compulsion. Tactics such as feigned sympathy, making false promises, or misrepresenting evidence can make an individual believe they have no choice but to cooperate, even if it's against their best interests.

These methods can result in false confessions or statements that aren't representative of the truth. For the justice system, this raises ethical questions about the means used to achieve a particular end. While the end goal of law enforcement is to solve crimes and ensure public safety, there must be a balance to ensure the means are just and don't violate an individual's rights.

The Duty of Law Enforcement to Respect Rights

Every individual has rights, and these rights must be upheld regardless of the circumstances. Law enforcement agencies have a duty not only to solve crimes but to do so while respecting the rights of the accused. Overstepping these rights can result in miscarriages of justice, where innocent individuals are wrongfully convicted.

The importance of this duty is underscored in landmark cases like Miranda v. Arizona and Missouri v. Seibert, where the U.S. Supreme Court set important precedents about the rights of individuals in custody.

Miranda v. Arizona (384 U.S. 436, 1966)

This landmark case changed the landscape of police interrogations. In a 5-4 decision, the Supreme Court held that suspects in custody must be informed of their rights to remain silent and to have an attorney present during interrogations. The ruling emphasized the inherent pressures of the interrogation room and the need to safeguard an individual's Fifth Amendment rights against self-incrimination.

Commonly known as the 'Miranda Rights,' this ruling has since been a staple in U.S. law enforcement procedures. It enforces the idea that individuals should be made fully aware of their rights and the potential implications of their statements.

The first line of your 'Miranda Rights' is telling. "You have the right to remain silent". That says it all right there. If it is the first thing an officer tells you, you should know it is important! So do it! Remain SILENT!

Missouri v. Seibert (542 U.S. 600, 2004)

Decades after the Miranda decision, the U.S. Supreme Court again delved into the world of police interrogations with the Missouri v. Seibert case. Here, the Court tackled the issue of the "two-step" interrogation strategy, where police would question suspects without giving Miranda warnings, get a confession, then provide the warnings and get the confession again.

The Supreme Court deemed this tactic unconstitutional, as it undermined the purpose of the Miranda warnings. It stressed that any confession obtained this way, without the accused being made fully aware of their rights, cannot be considered truly voluntary. Thus, any statement elicited without the officer giving the warnings would be deemed "inadmissible" in a court of law.

In Conclusion

The line between cooperation and compulsion is delicate and easily blurred. The justice system's integrity relies on ensuring that this line is not crossed, protecting both the rights of individuals and the pursuit of truth and justice.

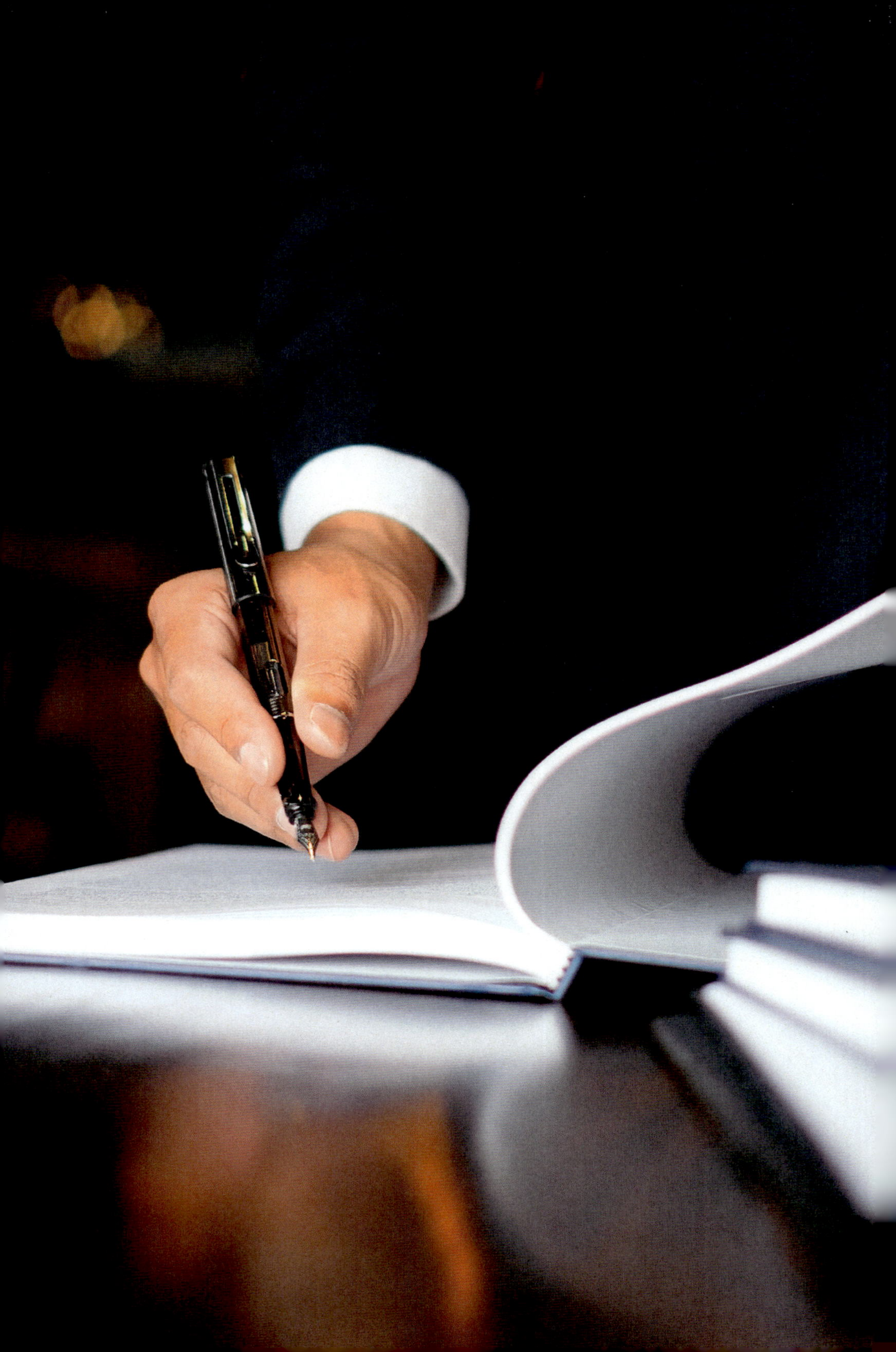

Chapter 5

THE ATTORNEY'S ROLE IN PROTECTING SILENCE

The Sixth Amendment and Right to Legal Counsel

The foundation of the American legal system rests on the principle that every individual has the right to a fair trial. Integral to this principle is the Sixth Amendment to the United States Constitution, which guarantees the right of the accused to the assistance of counsel for his or her defense in all criminal prosecutions. In essence, this is a safeguard that ensures that an individual, no matter the nature or gravity of the charges against them, has access to legal representation to navigate the complexities of the legal system.

Historically, the evolution of this right has seen significant transformation. Initially, the right to counsel was perceived merely as a right to hire private representation. However, as the landmark decision in *Gideon v. Wainwright* (1963) clarified, the state has an obligation to provide counsel to defendants in criminal cases who cannot afford to hire an attorney, recognizing the foundational importance of effective representation in preserving the integrity of the justice system. Thus, you have a right to an attorney at all stages, and if you cannot afford an attorney, one will be appointed for you, at no cost to you. This "appointed" counsel is sometimes called "the Public Defender".

Now, there are many GREAT public defenders out there. But, like any other profession, there are those who are not so great. Those with less education and experience than others. The good news about the public defender is you don't have to pay them. The bad news about the public defender is that you do not get to "self-pick" your attorney. You get the attorney that is appointed to you by the state.

Safeguarding Clients During Interrogations

One of the most pivotal aspects of the attorney's role begins even before trial – during police interrogations. While Miranda rights, derived from the *Miranda v. Arizona* (1966) decision, ensure that every person in custody is informed of their rights to remain silent and to have an attorney present, it is often the attorney's presence that makes a tangible difference.

A common misconception among the general public is that only guilty individuals request lawyers during interrogations. However, the truth is far from this. Interrogations can be intense, high-pressure situations. The primary objective of law enforcement during these sessions is to extract confessions, which might sometimes lead to aggressive or misleading tactics.

An attorney acts as a buffer in these situations:

1. **Ensuring Understanding**: They make sure their client understands the rights they have, such as the right to remain silent and not incriminate themselves.

2. **Protecting Against Coercion**: They ensure that the interrogation tactics used by law enforcement are lawful and not coercive.

3. **Advising on Responses**: They can provide advice on whether or not a client should answer specific questions.

Simply put, an attorney in the interrogation room isn't merely a passive observer. They actively shield their client, ensuring that the principles enshrined in the Fifth and Sixth Amendments are upheld.

Effective Legal Representation in Action?

To understand the importance of an attorney's protective role, consider the case of a man, we will call him Jonathan Clay. In 2017, Clay, a 20-year-old college student, was suspected of a series of burglaries. Though he maintained his innocence, the circumstantial evidence was significant.

During the initial hours of his detention, Clay was subjected to an intense line of questioning. Confused and scared, he made a series of inconsistent statements, which the police were keen on using as confessions and statements against interest.

It was only when his attorney intervened that the tide began to shift. The attorney demanded to review the footage of the interrogation and found that officers had employed deceptive tactics, convincing Clay that they had overwhelming evidence against him, even though they didn't.

Armed with this information, Clay's lawyer was able to argue in court that the so-called "confessions" were coerced and should be inadmissible. The case against Clay weakened, and a few months later, another individual was arrested and charged with the burglaries.

Clay's story is not unique. It emphasizes the critical role attorneys play in safeguarding the rights of their clients. From the interrogation room to the courtroom, their vigilant protection of the right to silence and effective representation can be the difference between justice served and a miscarriage of justice.

Did this guy do the right thing or not?

A True story of what "not" to do.

There was a young college student probably 21 years old. Let's call him "Dave".

Dave was working as an assistant manager at bowling alley. He was working his way through college, paycheck to paycheck. Money was tight. But Dave was also a criminal justice administration major and had aspirations to be a police officer. He had an inner compass and moral character, and he would NOT steal.

However, while Dave was working one night, one of the other employees was busy climbing through a drop ceiling and breaking into the boss's office. There was a small safe that was opened, and an unknown amount of cash was taken. The owner was convinced it was Dave. And the police were too.

Dave had nothing to do with the crime, but he was suspected, and there was circumstantial evidence that he "could have" done it. A detective reached out to him and questioned him. The detective used certain tactics, trying to convince Dave that he had information against him. The detective told him he had a witness. The detective told him he had his fingerprints. The detective explained to Dave that if he just admitted the crime and told his story, the detective would help him with the district attorney. The truth was, the detective didn't have any of those things. He only had a Victim that suspected Dave. That's it! Nothing else!

Dave didn't have money for a lawyer. He was literally "paycheck to paycheck". But what he did have was two things: One, a determination to prove his innocence. And two, the truth.

He met with the detective, and did a complete interview. He offered to take a lie detector test. And he threw himself at the mercy of this detective with the truth. He did absolutely EVERYTHING I am telling you in this book NOT to do!

In the end, the detective believed Dave. (The owner of the bowling alley? Not so much!) The detective agreed there was not enough evidence to charge Dave, and despite the strong feelings of the owner of the bowling alley, the detective recommended that the case be closed as "unsolvable".

Clearly this is a personal story from my past. It is all true. Had I fallen for the tactics of that officer, I could have been charged with a crime that I did not commit. And my whole future would have been altered. Heck, you would not even be even reading this book. But, despite the fortunate outcome of this huge mistake I made in talking to the police, I still recommend that you DO NOT DO THAT!

They never caught the individual who committed that crime. But to this day I still know who it was (Or I should say, who I *think* it was).

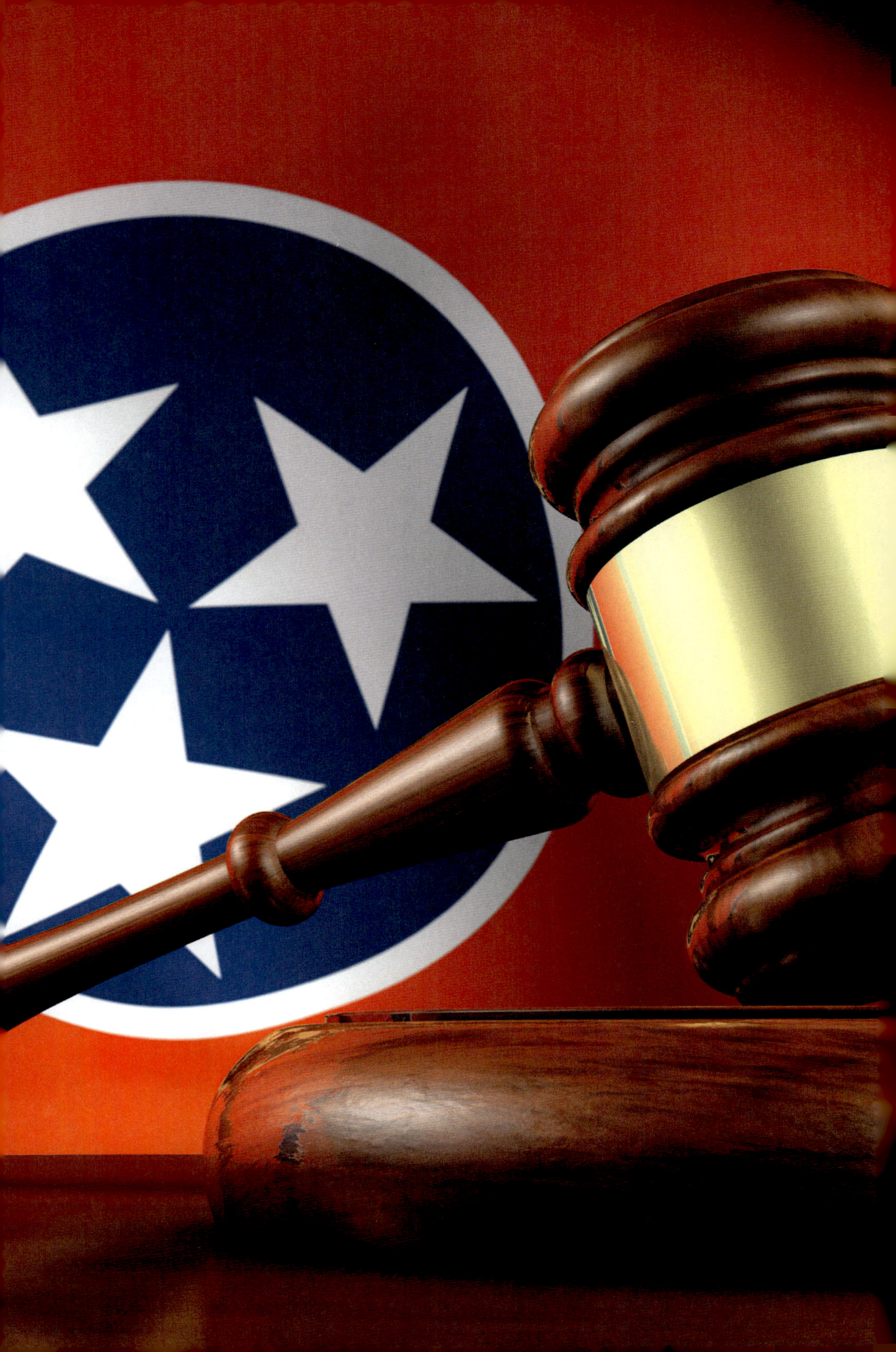

Chapter 6

THE TENNESSEE CONSTITUTION AND YOUR RIGHTS

I'm obviously a Tennessee lawyer. Everything I teach is based upon Tennessee law. The Tennessee Constitution is similar to its federal counterpart. The rights and protections it gives are basically the same. But it is your duty to read and understand it. While it may be required by caselaw for the police to formally advise you of certain rights before they interrogate you, it is still your job to know those rights anyway. Knowing these rights can help protect you and your family from a tyrannical government.

And, you know what they say about "ignorance of the law". It's no excuse!

The State's Duty to Protect Individual Rights

At the heart of any democratic society lies the duty of the state to protect individual rights. Without such protections, the very fabric of democracy can be torn apart. The Tennessee Constitution is no exception to this rule. While the U.S. Constitution lays the foundation for the protection of civil liberties at the national level, state constitutions like Tennessee's often delve deeper into the specifics of how these rights are to be safeguarded within state borders.

The commitment to ensuring that citizens are not subjected to the whims of an unchecked government is evident in both the language and intent of the Tennessee Constitution. To understand this commitment, one need only look at the enumerated rights and protections within this brilliant document.

Article I, Section 9: Protections against Self-Incrimination

Article I, Section 9 of the Tennessee Constitution clearly spells out protections against self-incrimination. The section states: "That in all criminal prosecutions, the accused hath the right to be heard by himself and his counsel; to demand the nature and cause of the accusation against him, and to have a copy thereof, to meet the witnesses face to face, to have compulsory process for obtaining witnesses in his favor, and in prosecutions by indictment or presentment, a speedy public trial, by an impartial jury of the county in which the crime shall have been committed, and shall not be compelled to give evidence against himself."

This provision is similar to the Fifth Amendment of the U.S. Constitution, which states that no person "shall be compelled in any criminal case to be a witness against himself." However, the Tennessee Constitution provides a more exhaustive list of rights of the accused, ensuring a more comprehensive protection against potential abuses.

A Comparative Analysis: U.S. vs. Tennessee Constitution

When examining the U.S. Constitution in comparison to the Tennessee Constitution, there are several key differences and similarities to note:

1. **Breadth of Rights:** Both constitutions have a Bill of Rights that guarantees fundamental freedoms. However, the Tennessee Constitution, like many state constitutions, often provides more specific details and protections than the broader language of the U.S. Constitution.

2. **Protection against Self-Incrimination:** As mentioned above, while both constitutions protect individuals from self-incrimination, the Tennessee Constitution offers more specific rights for the accused during trials.

3. **Flexibility vs. Specificity:** The U.S. Constitution is designed to be more adaptable and general, allowing for interpretation and adaptation over time. On the other hand, the Tennessee Constitution's detailed provisions make it more specific in its protections but may also make it less flexible in the face of evolving societal norms and values.

4. **Amendments and Evolution:** The process of amending the U.S. Constitution is rigorous and rarely done. The Tennessee Constitution, on the other hand, has been amended several times, reflecting the state's evolving priorities and circumstances.

In conclusion, while the U.S. Constitution provides a broad framework for the protection of individual rights, state constitutions, like Tennessee's, often fill in the gaps with more detailed provisions. Understanding both is crucial to fully appreciating the rights and protections available to individuals within a particular state.

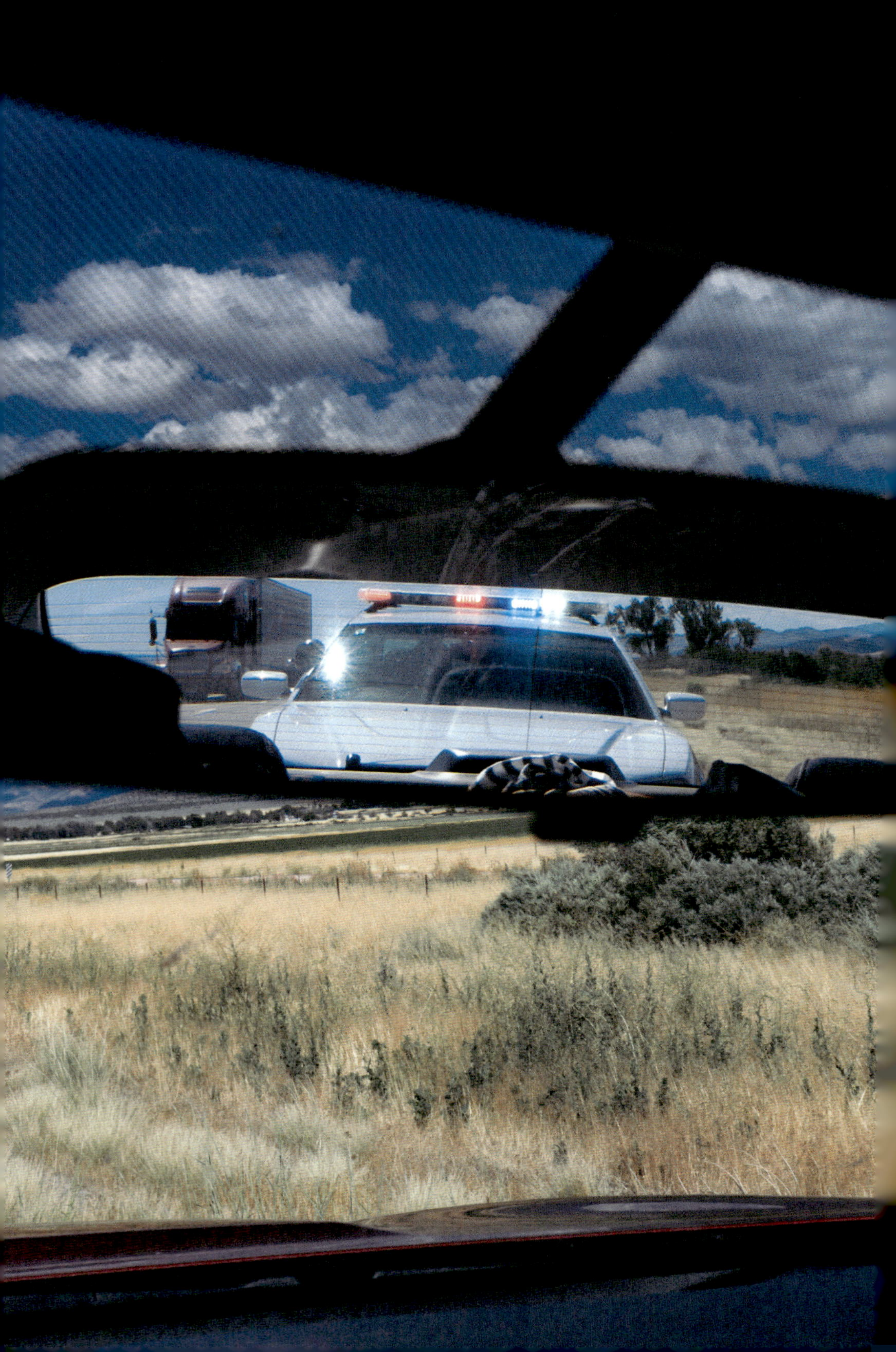

Chapter 7

PRACTICAL WISDOM: NAVIGATING POLICE ENCOUNTERS

Do's and Don'ts When Confronted by Law Enforcement

Interactions with law enforcement can be anxiety-inducing for many people. However, knowing your rights and understanding the protocol can reduce tension and ensure both your safety and that of the officer.

Do:

1. DO be polite and respectful.

2. DO remain calm and stay in control of your words, body language and emotions.

3. DO cooperate… but also **DO remain silent**. Cooperating does not mean consenting to tests or answering questions. Cooperating means be NICE and RESPECTFUL.

4. DO invoke your right to **remain silent**. That just means DO "shut up". Remember anything you say or do can (AND WILL) be used against you in a court of law. Everyone knows that right, most people can even recite it. But, few know how to invoke it. (And, how do you invoke it? You have to invoke this right **orally**. That means, you have to "say" it! You simply say "I don't answer questions without a lawyer". Period.)

5. DO keep your hands where the police can see them. If you have a weapon DO tell the officer immediately.

6. DO remain calm and still.

7. DO ask for a lawyer immediately upon your detention. Be sure to call an attorney that can be reached anytime of the day or night like Attorney David Ridings. Call my office for my cell phone. They will give it out freely day or night.

8. DO ask if you are free to go. If you're not under arrest or being detained, you have the right to leave. Politely ask if you are free to go. If they say yes, then walk (or drive) away.

9. DO Remember what happens and make a log as soon as you can. Try to remember what the officer tells you, and make notes immediately upon your release.

10. DO take photographs and/or video as soon as you are able. **If you are able to record the encounter, do so.** If the officer tells you to stop recording, politely refuse and say "I am recording for my safety and yours". If they tell you to stop recording and threaten arrest if you don't, then you

have a decision to make. But in Tennessee as in most states you have the absolute right to record police interactions as long as you don't interfere with their investigation.

11. DO take photographs after the encounter if you are injured. But, always make sure you seek medical attention first.

12. DO ask for an INDEPENDENT BLOOD TEST for drugs and/or alcohol. DO this if you are charged with DUI or Drug related stop. If the officer refuses, ask for his supervisor and make the request again. If they still refuse, make a note of that for your lawyer, and seek a drug/alcohol test immediately upon your release.

Don't:

1. **DON'T Resist Arrest:** Even if you believe you are being wrongfully arrested, it's essential to remain compliant. You can challenge the arrest later in a court of law.

2. **DON'T Give Consent to a Search Without a Warrant:** Unless law enforcement has a legal reason or probable cause, they may not search you or your property without your consent or a warrant. NEVER give that consent. Make them do their job and get a warrant if they have probable cause. Don't fall for the "we are going to get it anyway" lie that many officers will tell. Make them do their job.

3. **DON'T Make Incriminating Statements:** Remember the phrase, "You have the right to remain silent." Use it. Avoid answering questions without a lawyer present. As this

book tells you, only say **"I don't answer questions without a lawyer"**.

4. **DON'T Become Confrontational:** Arguing, shouting, or becoming aggressive can escalate the situation. It's essential to be respectful even when standing up for your rights.

Maybe:

1. **Identifying Yourself:** If asked, provide your name and/or show your ID, I would say **"maybe"** on this. It depends on why they are asking. If the officer has detained you for reasonable suspicion of a crime, then yes, you are required to identify yourself. Otherwise, Tennessee is not a "stop and identify" state. Cops can't just stop anyone and ask for ID. Even though many of them will tell you that they have that authority because they have to write a report and they *"need to know who they are talking to"*. No they don't. Don't fall for that. In order for the police to *ask* you for ID, they are required to have *"reasonable articulable suspicion"* of a crime. What does "that" mean? It just means that have to suspect you of either committing, or being about to commit a crime …and then they must be able to "articulate" why. (Articulate: Just means to speak, express, or simply "say" why they suspect you of a crime).

If a police officer asks for your ID, you are allowed to ask them if you are being detained. If they say yes, then you may be required in Tennessee to comply with the request for identification. If they say "no", then just walk away. You are NOT required to talk to a police officer for any reason. Most people have a problem with that. Most people in a civilized society are trained to "respect" authority. Most are trained to cooperate with police.

But, in all instances, your "speaking" to police should stop there. Even if you do identify yourself, you should never answer any other questions without a lawyer.

The Importance of Legal Literacy in Society

Legal literacy goes beyond just understanding laws; it's about grasping how laws apply to everyday situations and knowing how to use the legal system to protect oneself.

1. **Empowers Individuals:** With legal literacy, individuals can advocate for themselves and others, making them less vulnerable to injustice, or the wrath of a few bad cops.

2. **Promotes Trust:** When people understand their rights and the scope of law enforcement's power, it can help build trust between the police and the community they serve. Strengthening that trust is good for America.

3. **Reduces Unnecessary Legal Battles:** Legal literacy can prevent misunderstandings that lead to unnecessary legal battles, conserving both individual and societal resources.

4. **Strengthens Democracy:** A society where individuals are informed about their rights and the legal system is one where democracy thrives, as people can actively participate and engage with the system.

DUI Investigations Specifically

My general rule is to refuse ALL questions and testing if asked by police to do so.

There are very few and limited exceptions to that general rule, but what follows are my thoughts on the process and why you should refuse all testing on DUI stops specifically.

General Rule:

1. Breath and Blood – Always refuse UNLESS your POSTIIVE the results will be negative for drugs and/or alcohol. In other words, if you ***know*** you will be under the legal limit for alcohol and/or drugs in your system, then the results can help you. But this is a VERY limited scenario and not the norm.

2. Standardized Field Sobriety Tests – ALWAYS refuse

I am asked all the time about DUI stops. I have arrested, assisted in, prosecuted, and/or defended people in, quite literally, thousands of DUI cases. And the most common question I get as a defense lawyer is "should I take (or have taken) the breath test or blood test". Actually, most people already know they can refuse a blood or breath test. But what most people do not know is that they can also (and SHOULD ALSO) refuse the Standardized Field Sobriety Tests. But my advice can vary depending on the facts.

For example, if you think the chemical content of your breath or blood test will help you, then obviously take it. But that's not the norm in most instances. If I were stopped and questioned by police about a DUI, and I had not taken any medication or consumed any alcohol, then certainly I would want to prove the contents of my blood were not such that it would incriminate me. That test should help prove I'm not under the influence. But, on the other hand, if I had had a few beers and *wasn't sure about whether my blood would be over the legal limit*, then I would err on the side of caution and refuse the blood or breath test.

Now, I can hear you say, of course I would never be arrested if I had not consumed alcohol or taken medication, right? But you would be shocked how many people I have represented charged with DUI and gotten a blood test back to find NO ALCOHOL and NO DRUGS in their system at all! It does happen.

The standardized field sobriety tests (SFT's) on the other hand are a different story. I would ALWAYS refuse those. They are not given with an objective standard by which you are graded. In other words, there is no objective standard by which you pass or fail those tests. Officers will not say you passed them and they will not say you failed them. They will only say that you "showed indicators of impairment". So what does that mean? Good question.

There is not a "if you do this then you pass" or "if you do that then you fail". They are very "subjective" in nature, meaning they are whatever the officer determines in his mind after watching you perform them. You could have ten different officers watch the test, and get ten different scores on the indicators. That's not something I want to sign up for.

I am very black and white. If you tell me I go to jail if I put my foot down on this test, that's one thing. But that's not how these tests are graded, and that is not how they are instructed. The officer scores things you are not aware of as "negative" points against you. And every single thing that he scores as negative, is what your body would naturally do when in that situation. For example, if you tell me I'm going to jail if I put my foot on the ground, I may want to make sure I don't do that. I may use my arms like a tightrope walker to balance myself so I don't put my foot down. That's normal. That's natural. That's what a normal sober person would do. But in a DUI investigation, that is a point against you, meaning they call that an "indicator of impairment".

If you tell me I can go home if I don't put my foot down on this test, I may "hop" if I lose my balance so that I don't put my foot down. That's normal. That's natural. That's what a normal natural sober person would do. But nope! That's an "indicator of impairment" in the cop's report.

That's not fair! And those are not true indicators of impairment in my humble opinion. So taking those tests are not something I advise clients to do. Ever.

Now, there may be legal consequences to some of these choices. The police can charge you with an additional offense for refusing the blood or breath test (in some cases). That offense is called "Implied Consent" in Tennessee. It can be a civil charge, or a criminal charged depending upon the history of the person. But, there is NO LEGAL CONSEQUENCE to you refusing the standardized field sobriety tests. In other words, they cannot charge you with another offense for refusing the SFT's.

With that in mind, in my opinion the charge and/or offense of "implied consent" is worth the risk. Instead of providing chemical proof of an elevated blood alcohol level, I find risking the implied consent charge is a better choice in most cases. I would much rather fight the implied consent charge in court, than for a client to help prove the chemical content of their blood and lose on the DUI because of that test. And those implied consent charges are defendable for sure. In fact, I have found that we get the implied consent charges dismissed in a majority of the cases over the years. Sometimes those dismissals are in return for negotiations, and sometimes they what we call "on the merits" which means there was something wrong with the charge or the evidence thereof. But I have found I would rather fight those than for the client to give up his or her rights and submit to a blood or breath test.

In conclusion, practical wisdom in navigating police encounters is a combination of understanding one's rights, behaving judiciously, and being legally literate. As society works toward strengthening this knowledge, individuals can feel more empowered, protected, and aligned with the pillars of democracy.

You can help your lawyer defend you in court by making the right choices on the scene. But these decisions are tough. And they go against everything you were probably taught as a child in dealing with police authority. They go against human nature. Most people want to cooperate with authority (which is mistakenly translated as giving up your right to remain silent). That's exactly why I have written this book, so that I can help educate the general public on dealing with police contact and facing these choices. Now you can be one of the few who are aware of their rights, and actually know how to invoke them. Read on and learn more!

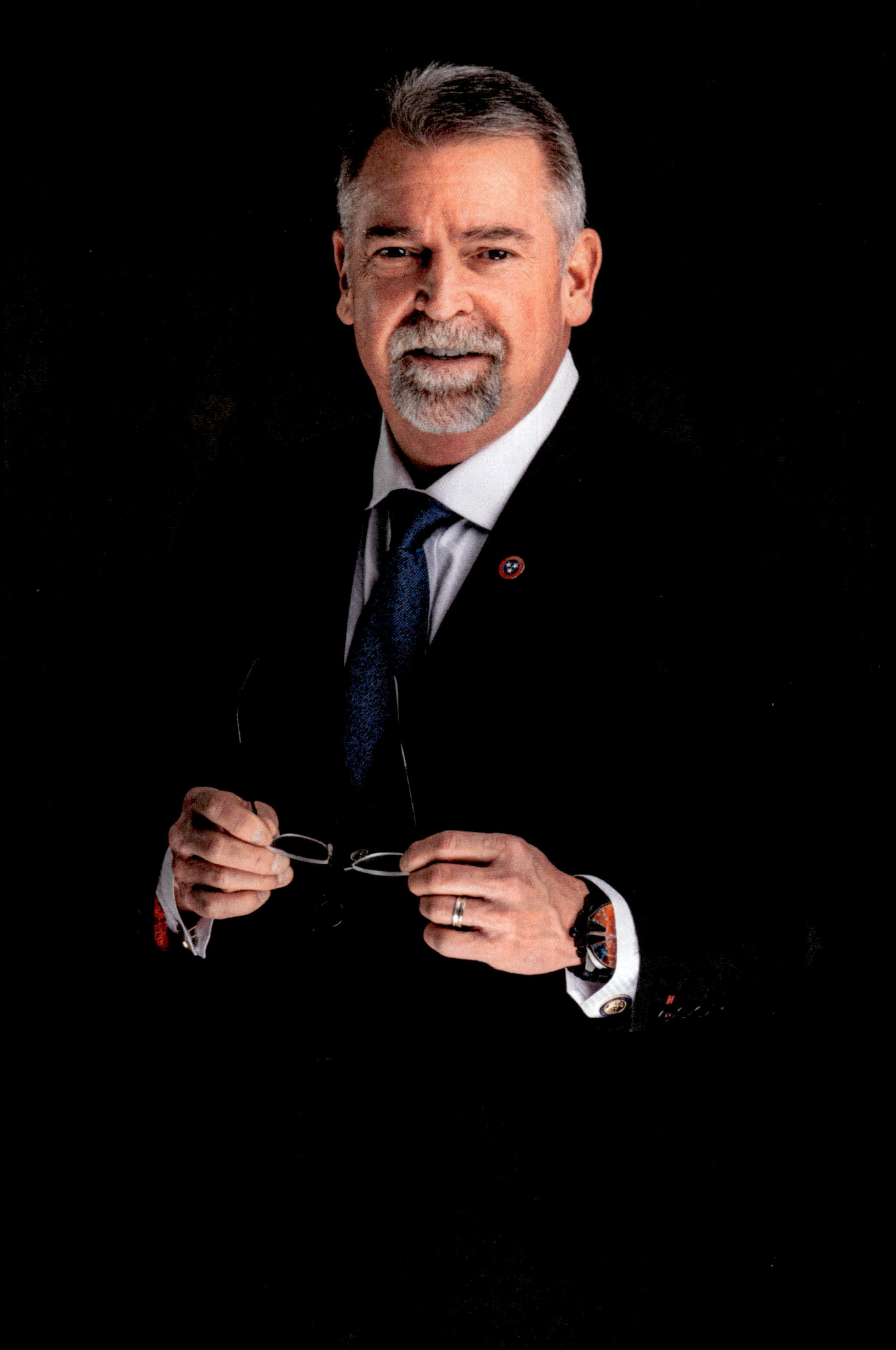

Chapter 8

REAL LIFE: TRUE STORIES FROM MY LAW PRACTICE

Every situation is different. I certainly cannot cover every scenario I have ever encountered in this book, but there is NO scenario I can think of where my advice would be different than the basic premise of this book.

Additionally, there is no way to predict how "not answering questions" will affect the investigation or the likelihood of you getting arrested. But I still believe that remaining silent is the key to protecting yourself from ultimate criminal conviction(s). There is no reason I can think of why I would advise someone to speak to police when questioned about a crime, unless "you" are reporting that crime. When police decide to investigate a crime, or they pull you over for a traffic offense, then everything they ask you has a purpose. And that purpose is to provide evidence against you so they can get an arrest warrant against you, convict you in court, and ultimately put you behind bars.

Don't fall for that.

The following case stories are true. The names and certain details may have been altered to protect the identity of the parties.

CASE NUMBER ONE

Soooo close!!!

I had a client who was arrested for DUI. We'll call him "John". When the officers first arrived, John was asleep at the wheel with his foot on the brake at a red light. It was a difficult situation for the police, because he had a loaded firearm next to his leg between the seat and the console. They positioned their vehicles blocking him in, so that he could not drive away, and began the process of waking him up. The danger was obvious, and the moment was tense. If he woke up startled and reached for his gun, he could have very likely been shot by police. But, he woke up easily, and without being startled. He was ultimately removed from the car without incident. The police did not immediately smell alcohol on him but obviously questioned him about drinking. He made the first mistake of admitting to drinking six hours earlier, and the investigation was on! But as officers continued their investigation and he made some very wise decisions (and also some key mistakes).

The police officer asked if he would "take a few tests to make sure he was okay for him to drive". [That's usually how they will put it. Don't fall for this trick.] John said, "I'm sorry, I was always taught not to take those test". That was the right decision, and the perfect way to answer that question. And officers did not know how to handle it.

They huddled up talking amongst themselves about what to do. The primary officer called his supervisor, and called a DUI enforcement officer who was not there, but was on shift. The primary officer told the others the situation and advised that this driver was unwilling to take tests. The primary officer told his supervisor that he did not want to arrest someone for "simply being tired" (which was honorable). But he had no evidence of impairment. He asked the driver at least three or four times if he would be willing to take test to make sure it was okay for him to drive. The driver politely refused each request. The primary officer called the DUI enforcement officer again, and asked his advice. The DUI officer advised the primary officer to "ask him **one more time**". He said, "**if he refuses again, then just take him home**".

This driver was about to go home! He was *one* answer of "no" away from going home.

What do you think happened? Well, you might have guessed that because I am telling you this story in my book, means that he hired me to represent him. Which also means he did not "go home". The officer asked him the last time and told John (lying of course) that the test "could only help him". The client fell for it and relented. He agreed to perform the Standardized Field Sobriety Tests. And, guess what? It didn't help him!

In actuality he did very well on the field sobriety tests. In my opinion, he should not have been arrested at all. I thought to myself, "man, he nailed those". But the officer having talked him into taking the test was able to check his little boxes (on his arrest report) and arrested this poor man. The man provided all of the "evidence" that this officer *needed* to arrest him. An hour later he sat in a jail cell waiting for bond. Had he told the officer "no" one more time, he would've gotten a free ride home. He was SO close!

This is an extreme situation, of course. It doesn't happen this way all the time.

In most cases, if you tell a police officer that you will not answer questions or that you will not take the standardized field sobriety tests then they will take you straight to jail anyway. But I have proof here that (at least in this case) refusing to answer questions and/or take tests would have helped this man significantly.

CASE NUMBER TWO

I don't believe I would have told that!

Client number two. We will call him "James". James was asleep at the wheel with his foot on the brake and the car in "drive". He was in the drive-through line at Taco Bell at approximately 2 AM.

He was detained and investigated for DUI, and unfortunately agreed to all testing and provided more than enough evidence necessary to arrest him. He took the all of the field sobriety tests, and did incredibly poorly on them.

While in the backseat of the car, the officer asked him if he would agree to take a breath or a blood test to determine the alcohol content of his blood. James responded politely. "Officer, let's say I've had 20… [short pause] … No, let's say I've had 25 beers today. Would it be better if I took this test tomorrow?".

The officer chuckled and said "yes, probably… But that's not an option here".

Then James made his first wise decision, as drunk as he may have been. He refused the breath and/or blood test, saying "No, thank you". Believe it or not, because of a technicality this case got reduced to a Reckless Driving with 6 month's probation and no jail time.

It pays to say "no thank you".

CASE NUMBER THREE

You want me to do what???

If a lawyer tells you to talk to the police… don't hire that lawyer! And, by all means you should question his/her advice. They are either a). ignorant of the law b). they just don't realize what cops do for a living; or c). they are trying to increase the odds for their retainer fee being paid. In any event, you don't want that lawyer.

I have a client. We will call him, Chuck. Chuck owns several businesses. He's an entrepreneur and a successful man. He owns houses in which he allows some of his workers to stay.

Two of these workers were pulled over for a minor traffic offense. During the stop, there was a quantity of drugs found in the car.

The police ultimately searched the home where at least one of the two defendants lived. That home was owned by Chuck, but Chuck was not in the car, nor was he at the house, nor was he involved in this investigation at all. Chuck owned this home, but he did not live there. He did not know that the drugs were in the home, and there is no evidence to suggest otherwise.

The police searched the home under questionable circumstances (of which have yet to be litigated) and found hundreds of pounds of marijuana.

The two individuals in the car were charged with various offenses regarding the drugs. But Chuck's name never came up. Neither of the current defendants have implicated Chuck in any way.

The police see that Chuck lives a "life of comfort" we will call it. But he has worked hard all of his life to achieve that life. And he is NOT a drug dealer. Now, the police may "suspect" Chuck of being a drug dealer. But there is no evidence to suggest he is involved.

Chuck went to see a lawyer because he was worried about the "optics" of him, owning the home where several hundred pounds of marijuana were found. The lawyer could tell that Chuck was worried and willing to pay anything to be protected. But, again, Chuck was not even a suspect. So the lawyer's advice to him should be simple. And originally it was. Originally the lawyer advised him to remain silent. "Don't say a word to anybody", the lawyer said. You are not a suspect currently despite what the police might "think". You have not been charged with any offense, and there is no known evidence that implicates you. And this was GOOD ADVICE.

But weeks later, the lawyer randomly called Chuck and advised him that he (the lawyer) was going to "set up a meeting" with the primary detective in the drug case (who the lawyer bragged was his "good friend".) [Now, pause here a minute and ponder to yourself, are you thinking what I am thinking?]

The lawyer convinced Chuck that, no matter what happened, he could "fix" any problems that arose because he and the detective were close friends. Chuck has the means to hire a team of lawyers should he need them. But there is not a charge pending, nor an investigation underway (of which we are aware).

But, the lawyer convinced Chuck that because of the lawyer's relationship with the detective the lawyer could "prevent him from being charged" no matter what Chuck were to say to the detective. But this new plan to meet with the detective did not give Chuck a warm and fuzzy feeling. Chuck was not involved in anything illegal, and did not want to "look guilty" by refusing to go to this meeting. But he was not familiar with his rights under the constitution and thought he "had to go". So Chuck planned on going and following the lawyers advice.

Prior to that meeting, and luckily for Chuck, someone told Chuck to consult another lawyer. One of my previous clients told Chuck to call me. "David has always advised us against talking to the police" they told him. "You may want to just ask David Ridings".

So Chuck came to see me. And as you might guess, I gave Chuck different advice.

Originally, this lawyer gave good advice. "Don't say anything to anyone". But now, he wanted Chuck to meet with the detective and talk to him? That is highly unusual. That advice causes the hairs on the back of my neck to stand a little bit (kind of like when you are watching a horror film and the tense music begins).

The lawyer wanted his client to meet with the detective and tell him all about his "alleged involvement" in, the drug trade… So that this same lawyer could "protect" him from being charged because of his "relationship with the detective"???

Believe it or not, this is a common story I am told by prospective clients. It has happened more than once. (Although not with the same lawyer, who still remains nameless).

Chuck insists that he has no involvement in the drug trade, and I believe him. But it made no sense for him to meet with the detective. My retainer fee to Chuck at this stage? "Zero dollars". I don't feel good about charging people to tell them not to talk to the police. Especially when they are not even a suspect yet.

There is no evidence to suggest otherwise, no warrant for his arrest, no pending investigation that we know of, and no witnesses who are saying Chuck was involved. Why did this lawyer change his strategy? I don't know the answer to that question. But it didn't feel right! Let's just leave it at that.

CASE NUMBER FOUR

Objection, your Honor!
Inadmissible self-serving statement!

This is a short story. I had a client who met with the police, gave a full statement before speaking to a lawyer, then hired me. We will call that client "Jim".

The damage had been done. All attempts to resolve this case without a trial failed. The state had more than enough evidence to proceed. And Jim had given them most of it!

When this case went to trial, it was a long and high-profile public trial. Jim had made statements that were in his best interest, and we wanted to admit those to the Jury at trial. The statements that he made that were probably things he should not have said (in other words, statements that were bad for his case) were ADMISSIBLE at every turn.

The statements he made that were good for his case were INADMISSIBLE at trial, and we were unable to talk about them at trial (unless we put Jim on the stand, which we were not sure we wanted to do at that point).

So. All that to say, keep that in mind that statements you make to the police during interrogation that are BAD for your case are always admissible. Statements that you make to police during interrogation that are "GOOD" for your case are always inadmissible… (unless you testify).

Why would you talk to the police with those rules? Good question!

CASE NUMBER FIVE

A real "who done it"!

I cannot give too many details on this case. But I had a client who came in charged with a crime where he and two others were charged. The victim didn't know which one of the three defendant's actually committed the crime, and the detectives were eagerly wanting to talk to all three of them.

One of the Suspects hired a lawyer that allowed his client to speak to the police. That defendant went in and made a few vague statements but said he didn't know who did the crime. Those statements confirmed he was there but did nothing to exonerate him. And it did not provide evidence against either of the other two. So, it was a futile statement. A waste of time. And a real danger to him, thus a mistake for him to go in.

I refused to allow my client to go talk to the police. They couldn't prove beyond a reasonable doubt that he was even "there". But they turned up the pressure. They called multiple times to try to get me to allow my client to speak to police. The district attorney called me personally and asked for a "favor". This DA said, "We don't suspect your client is the one that committed the crime, but we feel like he knows who did. Talking to the detective can only 'help him'."

But I said "nothing good comes from my client going in to talk to that detective". The DA disagreed, but we remained friendly. At the end of the day, the cases against my client were dismissed. Had we gone in and given evidence that even remotely tied him to the crime that would not have happened.

Some of the client's family wanted me to talk to the detective. They said "he is innocent, he needs to go tell his side of the story". They were advising the client to talk to the detective. But thankfully, the client was smarter than that and followed my advice.

Moral of the story: Never speak to a police officer about any crime, especially if you're innocent.

If you hire an attorney that suggests you go talk to the police officer, I would sincerely question that advice. There are one-in-a-million blue moons… But very few exceptions to my general rule: "never talk to the police".

CASE NUMBER SIX

> *If you let your client come in and talk to me, I'll help her confess to crimes that I cannot otherwise prove. And I will and help her get charged and convicted all over the Southeast United States with similar offenses.*
>
> *Really, I promise it's a good thing to talk to me.*

I have clients who are charged with shoplifting. The woman (we will call her Sue) was arrested in Middle Tennessee for shoplifting at a local store. The man (we will call him Trent) has yet to be arrested, but there is an outstanding warrant for his arrest. They are "suspected" of doing the same thing in many other states. They are suspected of going to a certain specific store across the southeast, and stealing tens of thousands of dollars of items. They have never been stopped or approached in any store. The store in middle Tennessee has warrants that allege Sue was seen on video stealing items, but she was not stopped at the time. Sue left the store unmolested and, other than this video, there is no known evidence of a crime. And I haven't seen the video yet. Trent was alleged to have been "at the store" and they believe acting as a "lookout". (very hard to prove).

In order to convict Sue, they have to have video evidence that shows definitively it is "her" and video to show "exactly" what was taken (to a degree beyond a reasonable doubt). The evidence necessary to convict Trent is much more complicated to explain. But neither of them have been caught "in the act" of stealing. And both claim they are 100% innocent. This case is still pending, and has not yet been litigated. I am not sure what the evidence is yet, as we have not filed discovery motions yet. That doesn't happen until the case goes to the Grand Jury and ends up in Criminal Court.

But the clients in the beginning were adamant about "wanting" to talk to the police. They were from a culture that believed they "had to talk to police" in order to tell their side of the story. They wanted to "explain" their innocence to the officer. They thought they could talk the officer into dismissing or otherwise resolving the case. But I explained that the detective did not have the authority to negotiate resolutions. The DA would have to be involved in that. And it was too premature for that process. My advice was to remain silent and NOT meet with the detective. And that remains my advice today.

But I believe that to be the best advice, as I doubt very seriously they have evidence in every store that 1) these people were even involved, or 2) what exactly was taken. Remember, the State must prove EVERY ELEMENT of the offense "beyond a reasonable doubt". That means that the must prove, not only that my clients committed the crime, but also "exactly" what was taken. Think about how hard that might be with only surveillance video footage from the respective stores.

The detective tried vigorously to get me to allow my clients to talk to him. He wanted them to admit they had been in these other stores in other states so he could charge them there. He claimed that he would "help" my clients with the DA if they talked to him, but he would charge them with more offenses if they didn't talk. Currently, no other jurisdictions have brought charges, and it has been more than enough time for them to have done so. So, I believe that the detective was lying about what he had as evidence. Imagine that!

I don't believe they have even video evidence of this couple stealing from any store. We will see what they have when we do "discovery". But until the state provides evidence against them in court, they cannot be convicted of any offense. The police officer can ATTEMPT to charge them in other jurisdictions (other states) but to do that he must have "probable cause" to prove they were actually "there" and that they "probably" committed that crime. To "convict" them he must have even MORE evidence and have it "beyond a reasonable doubt".

Probable cause is basically proving two things:

1. A crime was **probably** *committed, and*

2. YOU **probably** *committed it.*

Probable cause is a very low threshold of evidence. It doesn't take much evidence at all to charge someone with a crime. Equally, it doesn't take much evidence at all to "indict" someone at the Grand Jury level. Probable cause is VERY easy to make.

Also, many people don't understand that cops are *allowed* to lie to you during an investigation in order to get you to confess. It's not illegal for a police officer to lie to you, but it may be illegal for you to lie to a police officer.

Did you get that? It may be **illegal** for you to knowingly lie to a police officer, and impede their investigation. But a cop can lie to you *whilly-nilly*, and that's just fine?

Why on earth would anybody talk to the police given these rules?

Had the couple in this last example (either one of them) gone and talked to this detective, he could've (and likely would have) tricked them into believing they had evidence, and possibly tricked them into admitting things that would be otherwise impossible for him to prove. This has happened so many times in my career that there is not enough room in this book to tell the stories.

I wish more people knew they had the right NOT to talk to the police.

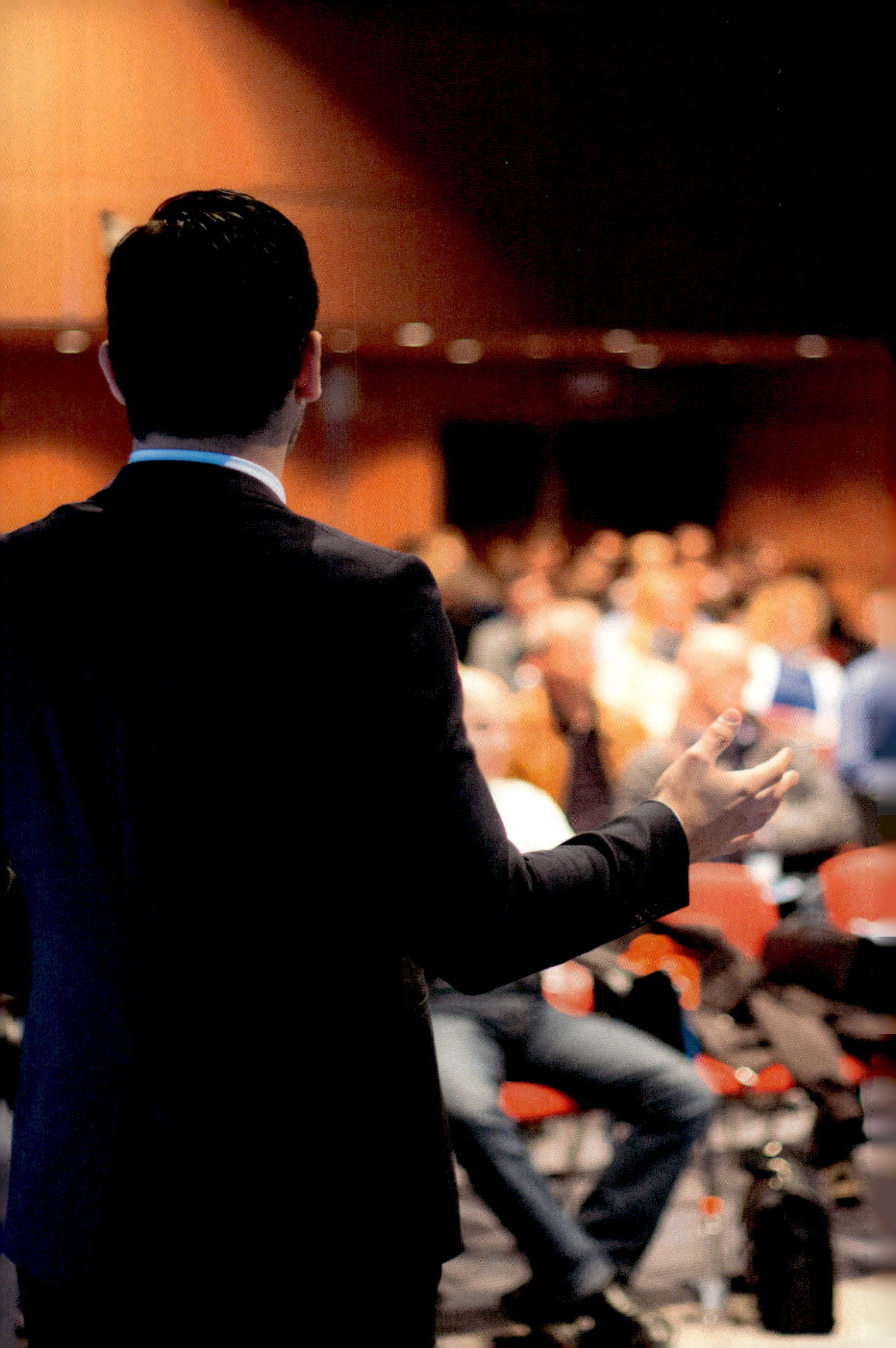

Chapter 9

WHAT NOW?

Educating the Public on Their Rights

Knowledge is power. While most individuals are aware of popular phrases like "You have the right to remain silent, anything you say can and will be used against you in a court of law" many are not fully aware of the scope of their rights during an encounter with law enforcement. My goal in writing this book is to "educate" people BEFORE they have a police encounter. Teaching people how to interact with police promotes safety, believe it or not. People invoking their rights under the constitution helps keep them safe, and promotes a calmer/safer interaction with police.

I'm not teaching anything that cops would not teach their own family. Cops know that people should not talk to them. And most cops agree with the information in this book. Most cops respect a person who invokes their right to remain silent, as long as it is done politely. While it may make their job harder, most officers respect those who know their rights and ultimately invoke the right to remain silent.

Community Outreach Programs: I do these all the time. Community Outreach Programs are designed to educate citizens on their rights. These programs might involve local lawyers, law enforcement officers, or community leaders providing seminars or workshops. YOU could become known as the expert on these issues. Just educate yourself on how to resist the interrogations of police, and why it is important to remain silent. Then go teach others what you have learned.

School Curriculum: Incorporating legal rights education into school curriculums ensures that young people are informed early. On your quest for information, you are reading this book. That's great, but continue on the path and get more education. Study your rights under the constitution and then teach others what you have learned.

Digital Platforms: Websites, apps, and social media can be leveraged to disseminate information about rights during police encounters. Short videos or infographics can be especially effective in conveying this information. Don't hide what you learn here. Use your platform to teach others.

Friends and Social Gatherings: Let's just be honest. You have friends. You have family. You may have friends or family who are prone to getting in trouble with the police. Even if you don't suspect they have those tendencies, everyone knows somebody who would benefit from having the information in this book. If you find the information in this book enlightening, or you have experienced the "pleasure" of a first-hand encounter with police, then teach your friends and family what you wish you had known before you encountered police. I teach every person who calls me "the basics" whether or not they hire me. From the first call, I always teach people about the mistakes they made during the encounter. I am always trying to teach people the things they wish they would have known the day before they got arrested or otherwise encountered police.

Your Responsibility

I am just one man. And unless and until this book hits the New York Times Bestsellers List, not a famous man. So, I'm enlisting you to help me spread this important word. Give someone this book, or at least tell them about your experience. Who knows… you may save someone from getting arrested and/or being convicted of a criminal offense. Like me, you could help enlighten people about their rights.

If you have had a real-life experience with police, then tell people about it. There is nothing to be ashamed about if you have been arrested. If you made mistakes that led to police charging and/or convicting you, something good can come from that. If you made some of the mistakes I have talked about in this book, then own it. And teach someone else what you wish someone would have taught you.

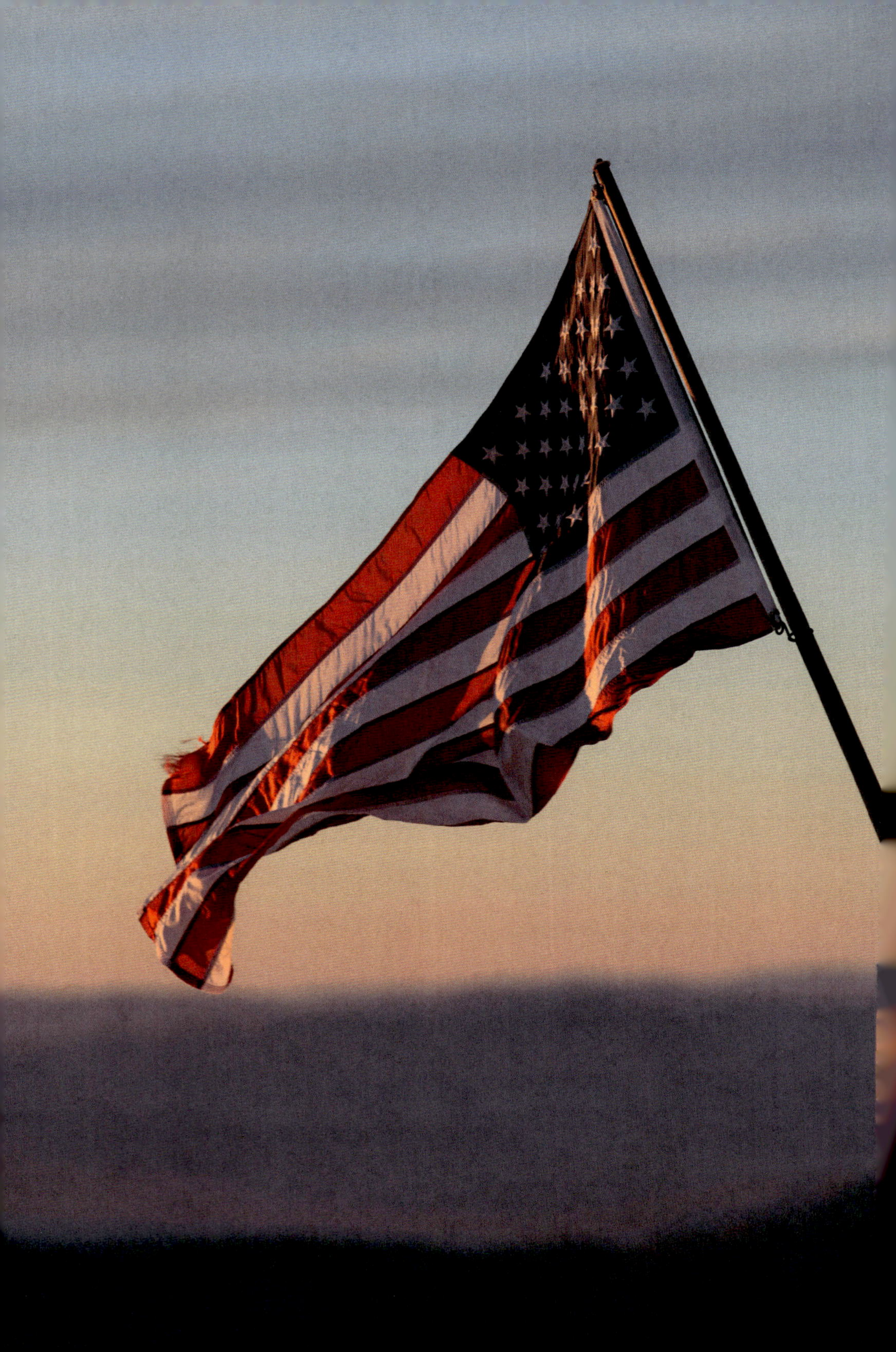

CONCLUSION

I love being a lawyer. Always have. My mother always said "David Glenn, you could argue with a fencepost". And she was right! I did have the gift of "arguing". Some people criticize criminal defense lawyers as though we "help people get away with crime". That's just not the truth. We don't defend "crime". We defend "the constitution". We protect the *process* for citizens who have to face this system.

Over the years I have met so many good people in my profession. There are, however, parts of my job that are disheartening. For example, meeting people in what most of them would describe as the worst time of their lives, and then having to teach them about all of the mistakes they just made… is hard. Especially when they come in feeling like they just made one of the biggest mistakes of their lives in the first place (meaning the event that led to them even needing an attorney like me).

But I believe if I don't teach them from the jump, then I'm not earning my money. If my advice doesn't start the minute they get me on the phone, then I'm not doing my job.

Most of my clients are what we call "one and done's". Meaning, they get arrested one time in their life and that's it! They are done! They never see me again. (And never "need" me again). Most would agree they don't *want* to see me again.

But … every now and then I'll get a repeat client. Sometimes, believe it or not, I will get a client that later gets arrested for the same thing as the last time. Usually a DUI. And, the first thing I ask them on the phone is, of course, "did you remember everything I taught you last time? Did you refuse everything? What did you tell the police?"

I love it when they say, "**I told him …I don't answer questions**"!

Sometimes

My greatest accomplishment is just keeping my mouth shut.